For all my dear loved ones,
past and present.

© Rayner Tapia, 2025

All rights reserved. No part of this book may be reproduced or utilised in any form or by any means, electronic or mechanical, including photocopying, recording, or by any information storage and retrieval system, without permission in writing from the author.

First published in 2025

Written by Rayner Tapia
Illustrated by Marian Marinov
Book design by Bryony Simmonds

ISBN: 978-1-915495-80-8 (hardcover)

Heartstone House Ltd
2 Bank House, Wark,
Northumberland, NE48 3LT, UK
info@heart-stone-house.co.uk

DISCLAIMER: The *Harry the Hedgehog* series is a work of fiction intended for children. Any resemblance to real persons, living or deceased, is purely coincidental. The characters, events, and settings in this book are products of the author's imagination and are not meant to represent any real individuals, organisations, or places.

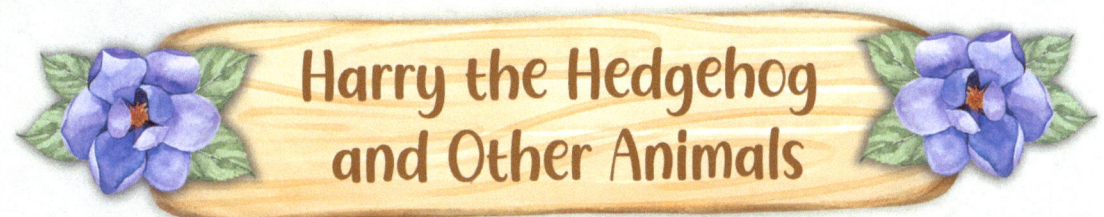

Harry the Hedgehog
and Other Animals

Harry the Hedgehog and the Lost Eggs

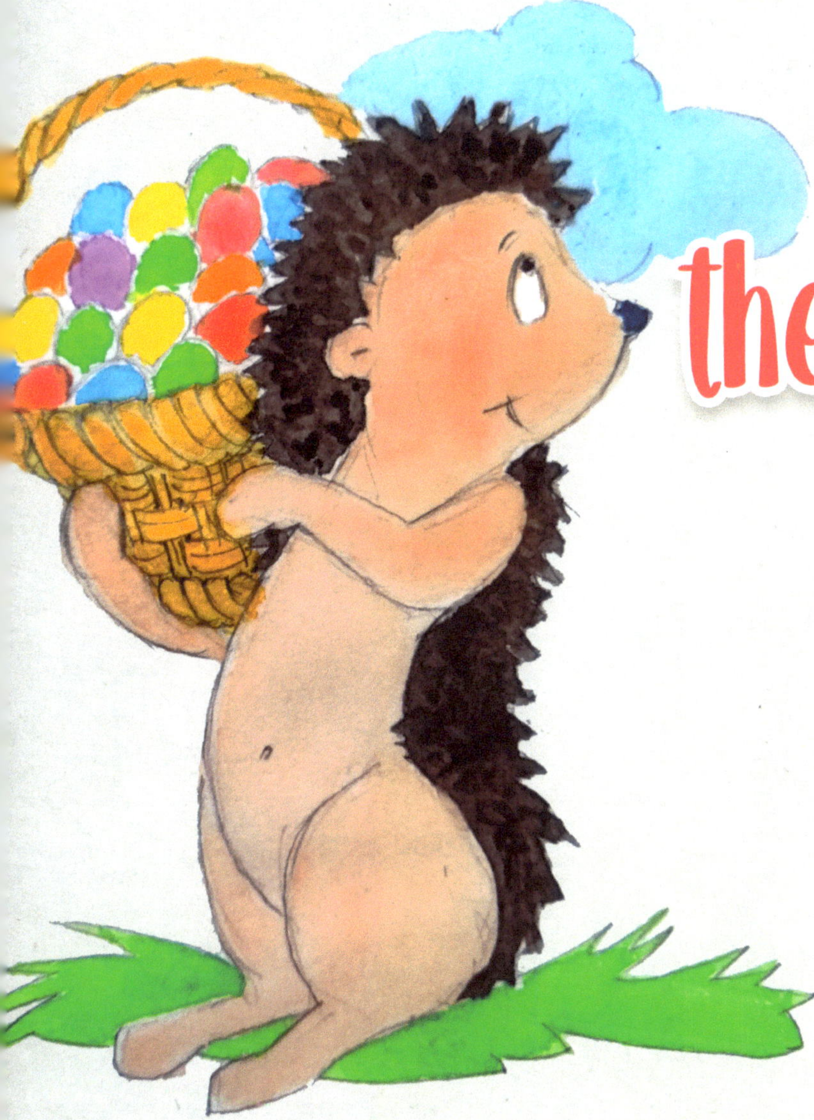

Written by
Rayner Tapia

Illustrated by Marian Marinov

Harry the Hedgehog was excited. It was Easter morning, and the forest was buzzing with joy.

Birds chirped, flowers bloomed, and a gentle breeze carried the scent of spring through the air.

But something was missing.

"Where are the *Easter eggs?*"

Harry wandered alone, his little nose twitching.

Russell the Rabbit hopped over, his fluffy ears flopping.

"Oh no!" he said.

"The eggs are missing!

I was supposed to hide them for the hunt, but when I went to get them, they were all gone!"

Milo the Teddy Bear Dog bounded up, wagging his tail.

"Don't worry, Russell!
We'll find them together!"
he barked.

Just then –

CLUCK! FLAP! WHOOSH!

A flurry of feathers burst from behind a bush. Out tumbled Clara the Chicken, her wings flapping wildly.

"CLUCK! CLUCK!

Oh, what a calamity! What a chaotic, catastrophic calamity!" she clucked.

Harry's spiky spines bristled and stood up straight.

"Clara, what's wrong?"

Clara the Chicken pecked at the ground nervously.

"CLUCK! CLUCK!" she squawked. "I was escaping from Farmer Joe's coop last night, and I saw someone sneaking off with the eggs. A striped furry tail flickered as it disappeared into the trees!"

Russell the Rabbit's nose twitched.

"Hmm," he sniffed. "A striped tail? That sounds like...

Cassie the Cat!"

Wise old Ollie the Owl, perched high in the great oak tree, hooted.

"Tweet-a-Hoo!

I saw Cassie the Cat scampering toward the hollow tree near the pond, carrying a full basket of something."

The friends rushed to the tree and **peeked into the hollow.**

There, curled up in a nest of grass, was Cassie the Cat happily nibbling at an Easter egg.

CRUNCH! MUNCH! LICK! YUM!

"So many eggs, all for me - mmm!" she meowed, licking her lips.

Cassie the Cat purred, flicked her tail, and licked her whiskers.

"Meow! Oh dear, was that today? I didn't know. I love Easter so much, and I couldn't resist these lovely eggs!" she meowed. "I'm sorry. Now that I think about it...

I suppose,
I did eat too many.

Milo the Teddy Bear Dog wagged his little tail.

"Woof-woof!" he barked. "I have a good idea. We can share what's left between us."

He looked at Cassie the Cat sternly. "But next time, ask before you take something that belongs to everyone."

Cassie the Cat purred.

"Meow, that sounds fair.

I'm really sorry!
I'll even help hide the eggs again
for the hunt!"

So, with Cassie the Cat's help, the friends returned the eggs to the meadow *just in time.*

Soon, all the animals joined in a grand Easter parade, playing games, hunting for eggs, and *sharing delicious treats.*

The garden was filled with laughter and joy. They ran, they played, they danced among the flowers. They were all delighted by the

magical Easter celebrations.

Even Cassie the Cat was careful not to sneak another egg -

she had learned her lesson!

Besides, her tummy was a little sore after her greedy feast!

The sun began to set, *casting a golden light* over the cheerful scene.

Wise Old Ollie the Owl perched on his favourite branch, watched over them.

"Easter is not just about eggs," he hooted softly. "It's about kindness, sharing, and thinking of others."

Harry the Hedgehog and his friends nodded, their hearts full of joy.

As they sat together, they shared their *favourite moments* from the day.

Russell the Rabbit laughed, "Next time, I think I'll keep a closer eye on the eggs!"

Cassie the Cat smiled.

"**And I promise I'll ask** before taking something that belongs to everyone."

Ollie the Owl fluttered down from his perch and smiled at his friends.

'Real happiness comes from thinking of others and sharing," he hooted.

"Kindness is even sweeter than Easter Eggs!"

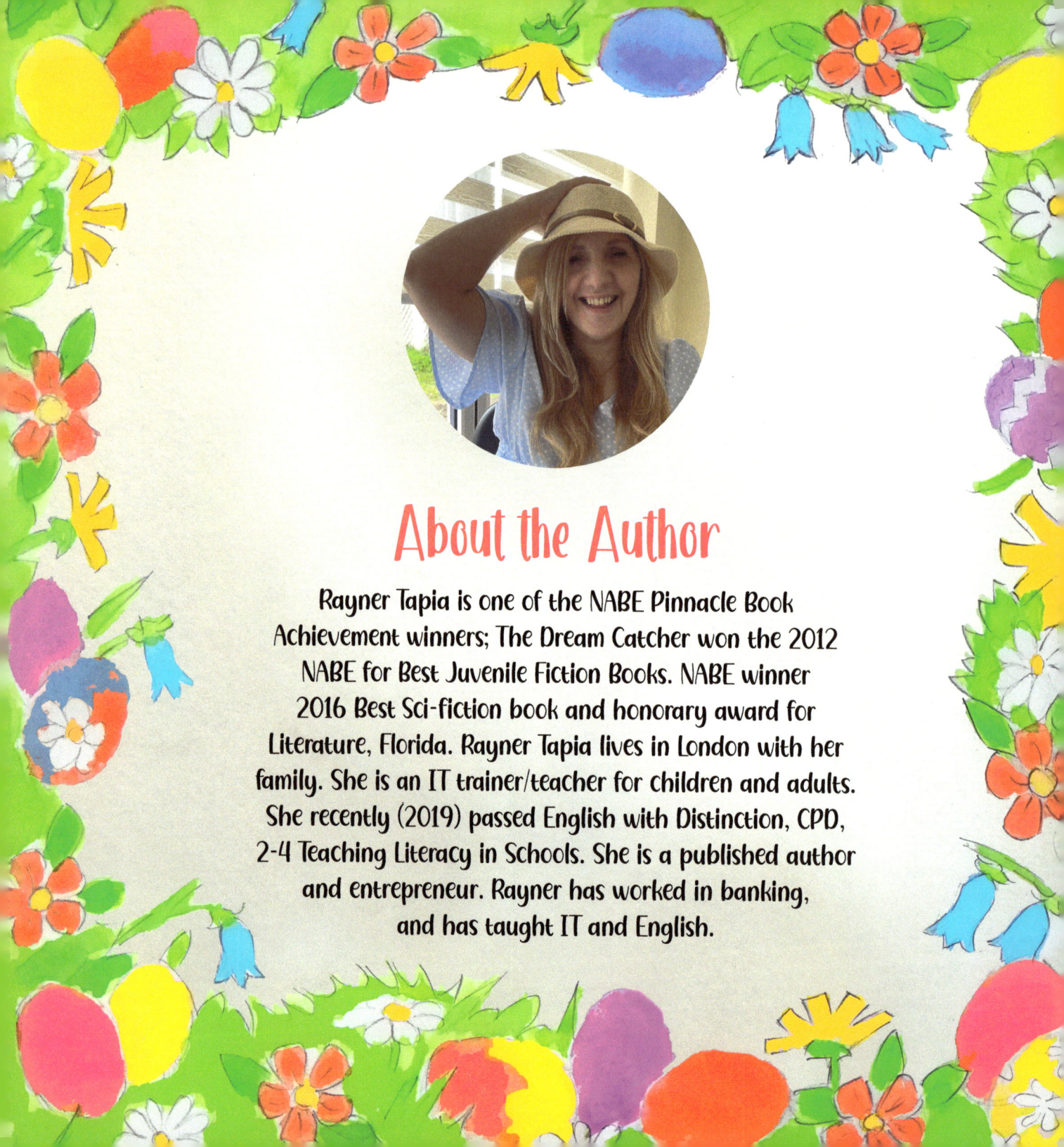

About the Author

Rayner Tapia is one of the NABE Pinnacle Book Achievement winners; The Dream Catcher won the 2012 NABE for Best Juvenile Fiction Books. NABE winner 2016 Best Sci-fiction book and honorary award for Literature, Florida. Rayner Tapia lives in London with her family. She is an IT trainer/teacher for children and adults. She recently (2019) passed English with Distinction, CPD, 2-4 Teaching Literacy in Schools. She is a published author and entrepreneur. Rayner has worked in banking, and has taught IT and English.

Other books by the Author

The Mouse Series

The Mouse and the Fox
The Mouse and the Christmas Tree
The Mouse and the King's Birthday Cake
The Mouse, the Llama, and the Sheep
The Mouse and the Bear
The Mouse and the Seal
Mouse goes on Safari
The Mouse and the Zebra
The Mouse goes Home
The Mouse is a Friend indeed

The Harry the Hedgehog Series

Harry the Hedgehog Saves the Day
Harry the Hedgehog meets Danny the Dog
Harry the Hedgehog meets Charlie the Crane
Harry the Hedgehog and the Missing Pumpkin
Harry the Hedgehog and the Fireworks
Harry the Hedgehog's Christmas Cheer
Harry the Hedgehog's Harvest

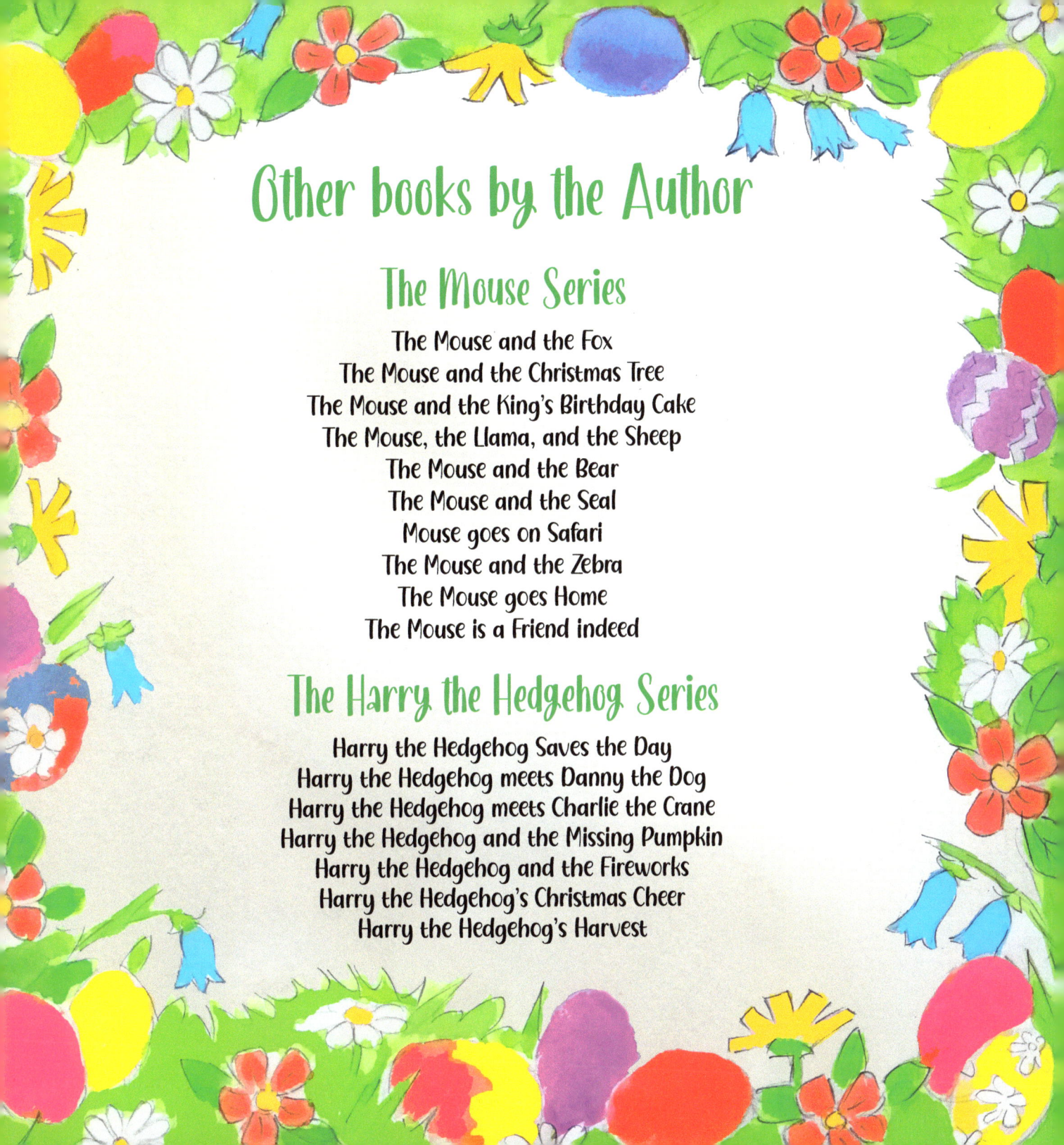

www.ingramcontent.com/pod-product-compliance
Lightning Source LLC
Chambersburg PA
CBHW041500220426
43661CB00016B/1210